What's in this book

This book belongs to

_____

颜色真好玩 Colour fun

学习内容 Contents

沟通 Communication

说说颜色
Talk about colours

背景介绍：
男孩拿着水彩调色盘
正在调色。

生词 New words

★ 红色　red

★ 黄色　yellow

★ 蓝色　blue

★ 绿色　green

★ 黑色　black

★ 白色　white

★ 灰色　grey

★ 吗　(question word)

　颜色　colour

句式 Sentence patterns

这是黄色吗?
Is this yellow?

你喜欢绿色吗?
Do you like green?

跨学科学习 Project

认识动物保护色及
具有变色能力的动物
Learn about camouflage and
colour-changing animals

文化 Cultures

红色在中国文化中的意义
The colour red in Chinese culture

参考答案:
1 There are four colours on the palette: blue, red, green and yellow.
2 Mixing different colours together will make a different colour.
3 My favourite colour is red/blue/yellow.

Get ready

1 How many colours are there on the palette?

2 What happens when different colours are mixed?

3 What is your favourite colour?

故事大意：
本课介绍了不同颜色，以及不同颜色混合以后会变成其他颜色。

教学活动建议：
可以让学生在调色盘上根据课文内容一边学习一边体验，加强理解，提高学习效率。

huáng sè
黄色

这是黄色吗？

参考问题和答案：
What colour is on the canvas? (It is yellow.)

lán sè

蓝色

黄色加蓝色，颜色会变吗？

参考问题和答案：

1. What colour is on the brush? (It is blue.)
2. Do you think mixing yellow and blue will make a different colour?
   (Yes, I think yellow mixed with blue will make a different colour./
   No, I do not think so.)

lù sè
绿色

黄色加蓝色，会变成绿色。

参考问题和答案：
What colour will mixing yellow and blue make? (Mixing yellow and blue will make green.)

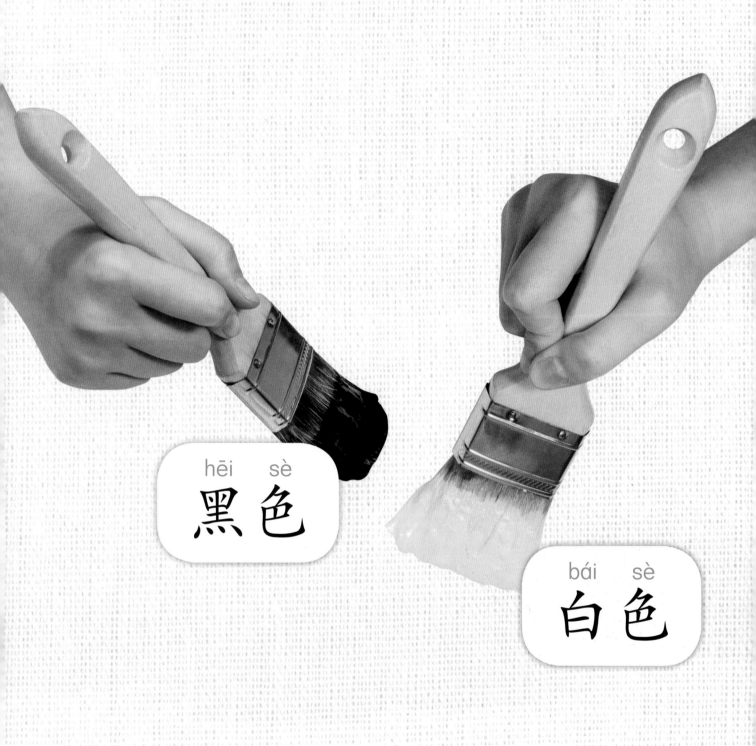

hēi sè
黑色

bái sè
白色

黑色加白色，变成什么颜色？

参考问题和答案：

1　What colours are on the brushes? (There is black on the left brush and there is white on the right brush.)

2　Do you think mixing black and white will make a different colour? (Yes, mixing black and white will make a different colour./No, I think black will cover up the white.)

huī sè
灰色

黑色加白色，变成灰色。

参考问题和答案：

What colour will mixing black and white make? (Mixing black and white will make grey.)

hóng sè
红色

参考问题和答案：
1 What colour is on the left brush? (Red.)
2 What colour do you think will mixing red, blue and green make? (I think it will be brown./I have no clue.)

红、蓝、绿在一起，变成什么颜色？

Let's think

1 **Look at the colour mixing picture and think. Put a tick or a cross.**

提醒学生回忆故事，观察第6、8两页，也可以让学生自己实践调色后验证答案。

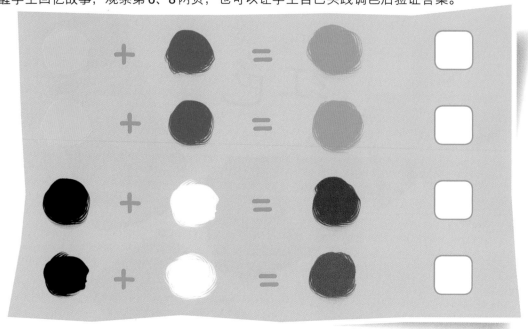

2 **What colour do you get when mixing red, blue and green together? Try it out on the dinosaur.**

I think it will be black.

老师提醒学生先在调色板上混合调色，最后将调好的颜色涂在恐龙身上。

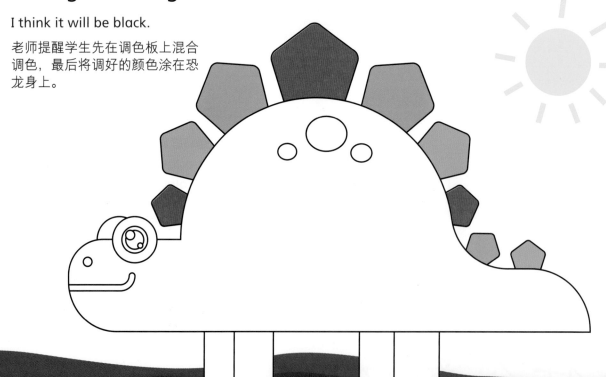

10

New words

02 **1** Learn the new words.

灰色　吗　黑色　白色　黄色　红色　绿色　蓝色　颜色

2 Match the words to the pictures. Write the letters.

a 红色　b 绿色　c 蓝色　d 黑色　e 黄色　f 白色　g 灰色

可以让学生一边填字母，一边说出海星的颜色。建议句式："它是……色的。"

听听说说 Listen and say

 1 Listen carefully. Put a tick or a cross.

 2 Look at the pictures. Listen to the st...

第二题参考问题和答案：

Why does the magician show the yellow handkerchief?
(Because Ivan said yellow is his favourite colour.)
Have you ever seen a magic show? Did you like it?
(Yes, I saw a wonderful magic show with my parents
last year. I love magic shows./No, I have never seen
a magic show before.)

d say.

3 Match and say. Colour the pictures.

先让学生根据问题来选择
合适的回答并连线，再将
图案涂上回答中所提及的
颜色。

Task

提醒学生仔细找，并勾出相应的颜色。完成后说出完整的中文句子与同学分享。

Tick the colours of the flags and say.

它有红色和黄色。

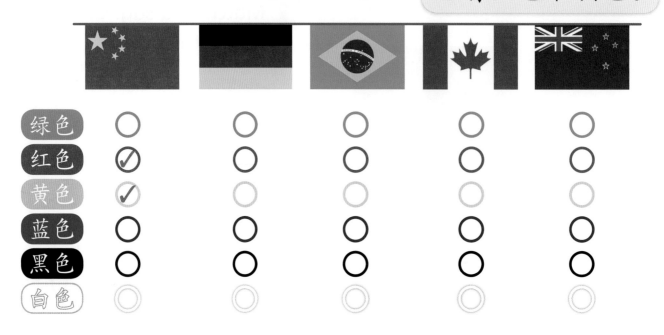

绿色	◯	◯	◯	◯	◯
红色	✓	◯	◯	◯	◯
黄色	✓	◯	◯	◯	◯
蓝色	◯	◯	◯	◯	◯
黑色	◯	◯	◯	◯	◯
白色	◯	◯	◯	◯	◯

Game

游戏方法：
学生两人一组，一人针对图画进行提问或者描述，另一人回答并指出相应的图片。

Work with your friend. Listen and point to the correct objects.

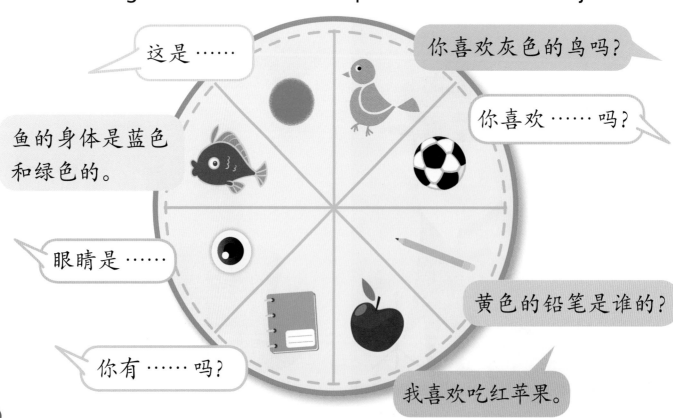

这是……

你喜欢灰色的鸟吗？

鱼的身体是蓝色和绿色的。

你喜欢……吗？

眼睛是……

黄色的铅笔是谁的？

你有……吗？

我喜欢吃红苹果。

Song

05 **Listen and sing.**

红黄蓝绿黑白灰，

红加黄，变成橙。

黄加蓝，变成绿。

黑加白，变成灰。

红黄蓝绿黑白灰，

变变颜色真好玩。

桔子或橙子
的颜色就是
橙色。

课堂用语 Classroom language

现在开始。

Start now.

涂颜色。

Colour the picture.

写一写 Write

1 Learn and trace the stroke. 老师示范笔画动作，学生跟着做：用手在空中画出"撇折"。

撇折

2 Learn the component. Circle 纟 in the characters.

红 绿 结 纸

"绞丝旁"像缠绕、打结的丝线。引导学生发现绞丝旁字与丝线、纺织和布匹等有关。

3 Circle the characters with 纟.

红 纸 结 线 绿 孩 黄 颜 鱼 蓝

4 Trace and write the character.

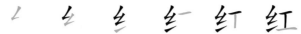

5 Write and say.

我喜欢  色。

 汉字小常识 *Did you know?*

Study the characters. Colour the meaning component red and the sound component green.

Many characters are made up of two components. One gives a clue to the meaning, while the other to the sound.

| 姐 | 妈 | 星 | 睛 | 绿 |

1 妈："女"表示女性，发音同"马"。　　2 星："日"表示发光的天体，发音似"生"。
3 睛："目"表示眼睛，发音近似"青"。　　4 绿："绞丝旁"表示丝，发音近似"录"。

Cultures

1 When you think of the colour red, what comes to your mind? Tick the boxes. 可以让学生说说联想到的其他与红色有关的物品。如：西瓜、嘴唇和枫叶等。

2 Do you know the meaning of red in Chinese culture?

Chinese Palaces

中国农历新年时，长辈会给晚辈发"红包"，象征新年平安好运。

Chinese New Year

Wedding

中国传统文化中，红色寓意庄严和吉祥，所以古代宫殿的主色调多为红色。

中国传统婚礼中，新郎和新娘会穿红色的礼服，象征吉祥如意。

> Red is a popular colour in China. It means glory, happiness and good luck. You see it a lot during Chinese celebrations and festivals.

除上述几种情况外，祝寿、开张和庆功等活动都会以红色作为主色。但是红色的使用也有禁忌，如不能用红笔写别人名字，表示该人已死或是即将行刑的死刑犯。

老师可以和同学们一起讨论题中动物变色的原因。还可以说说其它会变色的动物，如比目鱼、树蛙和岩雷鸟等。

1 Some animals can change colour to protect themselves. Read and write the letters.

章鱼受到惊吓或袭击时，身体会变成蓝色。此外，它会根据周围环境而相应变色，从而保护自己。

A B C D E F

Octopuses change colour to communicate with their friends or when frightened.

| A | 我变成灰色。 |

Chameleons change the colour of their skin to match the surroundings.

| B | 我变成蓝色。 |

| C | 冬天来了，我变成白色。 |

Arctic foxes change the colour of their fur with the seasons.

| D | 我变成黑色。 |

| F | 我变成绿色。 |

在冬天，北极狐的毛会变成白色，这样有利于捕食猎物和逃避被捕杀。

变色龙会根据周围环境变色，以更好地隐蔽和捕食，如变成绿色隐蔽于植物中。也会用体色表达情绪或身体状况，如身体发黑是身体状况较差。

2 Paint your hands and play with your friends.

我的翅膀是蓝色的吗？

我有灰色的长鼻子。

学生可以模仿书上的或自己将手扮成其它动物（如兔子、小鸟等），然后用手绘彩上色，最后用中文互相交流。

19

温习 Checkpoint

1 Look at the wheel and answer the questions.

游戏方法：

学生转动转盘，完成指针所指的相应问题，也可按数字顺序依次完成所有题目。

8 香蕉是什么颜色？

7 我有红色的身体吗？

6 Write 'red' in Chinese.

5 我的身体是什么颜色？

评核方法：

学生两人一组，互相考察评价表内单词和句子的听说读写。交际沟通部分由老师朗读要求，学生再互相对话。如果达到了某项技能要求，则用色笔将星星或小辣椒涂色。

2 Work with your friend. Colour the stars and the chillies.

Words and sentences	说	读	写
红（色）	☆	☆	☆
黄色	☆	☆	🌶
蓝色	☆	☆	🌶
绿色	☆	☆	🌶
黑色	☆	☆	🌶
白色	☆	☆	🌶
灰色	☆	☆	🌶
吗	☆	☆	🌶
颜色	☆	🌶	🌶
这是红色吗？	☆	☆	🌶
你喜欢绿色吗？	☆	☆	🌶

Talk about the colours	☆

色加什么颜色，
成绿色？

⭐2 我是蓝色
的吗？

⭐3 你喜欢什
么颜色？

⭐4 你喜欢我吗？

3 What does your teacher say?

评核建议：

根据学生课堂表现，分别给予"太棒了！(Excellent!)"、"不错！(Good!)"或"继续努力！(Work harder!)"的评价，再让学生圈出上方对应的表情，以记录自己的学习情况。

分享 Sharing

Words I remember

红色	hóng sè	red
黄色	huáng sè	yellow
蓝色	lán sè	blue
绿色	lù sè	green
黑色	hēi sè	black
白色	bái sè	white
灰色	huī sè	grey
吗	ma	(question word)
颜色	yán sè	colour

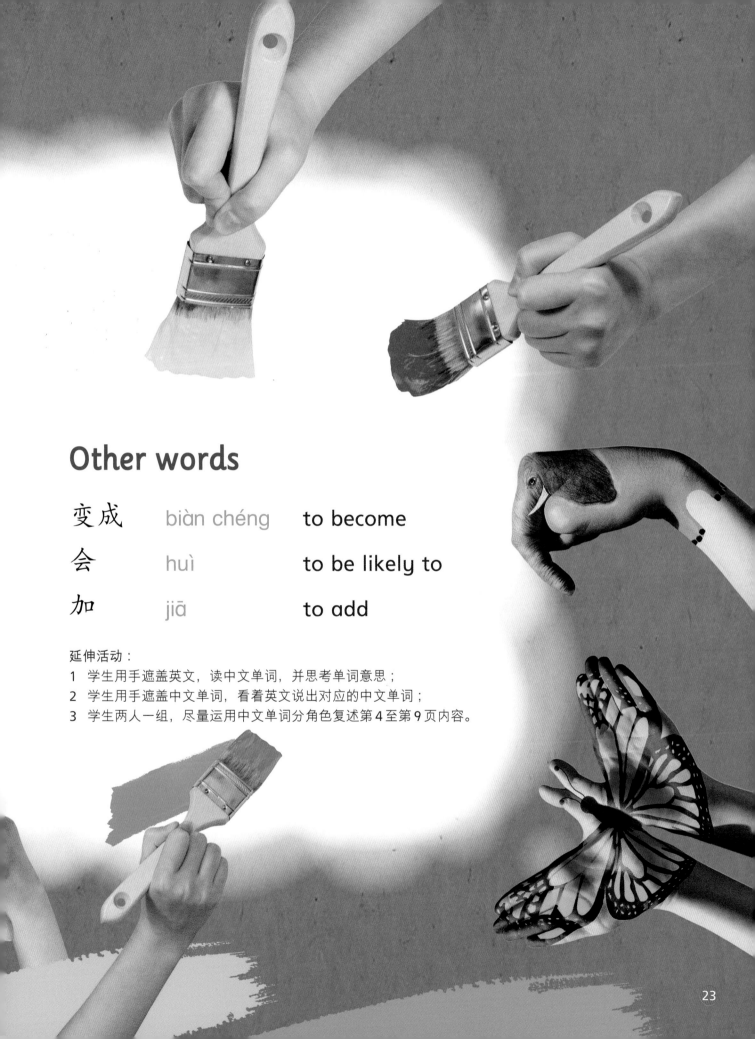

Other words

变成	biàn chéng	to become
会	huì	to be likely to
加	jiā	to add

延伸活动：

1 学生用手遮盖英文，读中文单词，并思考单词意思；

2 学生用手遮盖中文单词，看着英文说出对应的中文单词；

3 学生两人一组，尽量运用中文单词分角色复述第 4 至第 9 页内容。

Oxford University Press is a department of the University of Oxford.
It furthers the University's objective of excellence in research, scholarship,
and education by publishing worldwide. Oxford is a registered trade mark of
Oxford University Press in the UK and in certain other countries

Published in Hong Kong by
Oxford University Press (China) Limited
39th Floor, One Kowloon, 1 Wang Yuen Street, Kowloon Bay,
Hong Kong

Illustrated by Anne Lee and Wildman

Photographs for reproduction permitted by Dreamstime.com

China National Publications Import & Export (Group) Corporation is an authorized distributor of
Oxford Elementary Chinese.

Please contact content@cnpiec.com.cn or 86-10-65856782

ISBN: 978-0-19-082146-3

10 9 8 7 6 5 4 3 2

Teacher's Edition
ISBN: 978-0-19-082158-6

10 9 8 7 6 5 4 3 2